Your Financial Playbook

A Guide to Navigating the World of Personal Finance

By

Mark Riddix

Avid Readers Publishing Group
Lakewood, California

This is a work of non-fiction. The opinions expressed in this manuscript are those of the author(s) and do not represent the thoughts or opinions of the publisher. The author(s) warrants and represents that he/she has the legal right to publish or owns all material in this book. If you find a discrepancy, contact the publisher at www.avidreaderspg.com.

Your Financial Playbook
A Guide to Navigating the World of Personal Finance

All Rights Reserved

Copyright © 2010 Mark Riddix

This book may not be transmitted, reproduced, or stored in part or in whole by any means without the express written consent of the publisher except for brief quotations in articles and reviews.

Avid Readers Publishing Group

http://www.avidreaderspg.com

ISBN-13: 978-1-935105-54-1

Printed in the United States

Table of Contents

Introduction	V
Chapter 1: How To Build Wealth	1
Chapter 2: Understanding Savings and Money Market Accounts	5
Chapter 3: Investing In Certificates of Deposit & Savings Bonds	13
Chapter 4: Types of Retirement Accounts	19
Chapter 5: Introduction to Stocks	27
Chapter 6: The Art of Investing	39
Chapter 7: Shaping Your Investment Strategy	45
Chapter 8: Getting Started Investing	55
Chapter 9: Saving For Your Kids College	61
Chapter 10: Teaching Your Kids About Money	67
Chapter 11: Managing Credit	71
Chapter 12: Biggest Money Traps	79
Chapter 13: Money Saving Tips	85
Chapter 14: Money Making Ideas	99
Chapter 15: Great Financial Resources	101
Conclusion	109
Appendix	113

Introduction

How many people are interested in learning about making money? Everyone is! YOUR FINANCIAL PLAYBOOK is here to help you on your wealth building journey. YOUR FINANCIAL PLAYBOOK looks at all aspects of finance including investing, debt elimination, credit management, money saving tips, retirement planning, and teaching kids about money. This book will aim to bring clarity to the basic ins and outs of building wealth, investing, and saving money. This book will benefit anyone that is interested in learning more about money and finance. YOUR FINANCIAL PLAYBOOK takes an in depth look at savings accounts, money market accounts, certificates of deposit, stocks, bonds, mutual funds, retirement planning, IRA's, 401(k)'s, and college planning. There are a ton of useful tips about building credit the right way. This book will help you navigate the complicated world of finance.

YOUR FINANCIAL PLAYBOOK is the ultimate How-To Guide. You will learn about the vast array of investment products that exist and which ones are the best for you. You can take all of the financial principles discussed and apply them to your life. After reading this book, you will be well on your way to being financially responsible and building wealth! This book is a useful read for the finance novice and the seasoned investor. YOUR FINANCIAL PLAYBOOK aims to provide capital appreciation strategies for individuals seeking to build wealth. The book contains practical real life examples. You can learn from the author's pitfalls in the financial arena so that you can avoid making some of the same mistakes. The book also discusses specific books and online resources that will be useful in building your financial future. With all of these resources at your disposal, you will be well on your way to financial success!

Chapter 1:

How to Build Wealth

The Five I's of Building Wealth

There is no one method to building wealth. There are many different avenues to financial success. One of the easiest ways to learn about building wealth is by following the examples of people that have already built fortunes. Every year Forbes magazine publishes a list of the richest people in the world. Everyone on the list has amassed a great sum of money. While reading the list, I discovered that most of the billionaires listed fit into one of five categories. I call these categories the 5 I's. Below is a list of the five categories that make up the world's richest people.

1) **Investors**

Investors commit money to an endeavor with the expectation of profit. This can be through saving or purchasing an asset for capital gains. Warren Buffett has built his fortune through stock investing. Donald Trump made his billions by investing in real estate. Jerry Jones got rich in oil and gas exploration.

2) **Inventors**

These are the creators of a new good or service. You just have to see a need for a product that others do not see. James Dyson became a billionaire by developing the bagless vacuum cleaner. His idea was initially rejected because it was seen as hurting vacuum bag sales. Today the dyson vacuum is an international best seller.

3) **Inheritors**

This is the easiest path to wealth. You need rich relatives for this one though! Ask Jim Walton, S Robson Walton, Alice Walton and Christy Walton who are the 4th, 5th, 6th and 7th richest Americans. They are the heirs of the Walmart fortune.

4) **Innovators**

These are the people that develop a new way of doing things. You don't have to come up with the next great idea, just improve upon an existing one. Steve Jobs of Apple is one of the great innovators. From the iPod to the iPhone to the iMac, Apple is always on the cutting edge of innovation.

5) **Entrepreneurs**

Entrepreneurs are the risk takers that start and manage a business. Entrepreneurship can take many forms from purchasing a franchise to creating a start up. Bill Gates of

Microsoft and Larry Ellison of Oracle grew small technology firms into the world's largest software companies. Oprah Winfrey began her career in local news and is now the CEO of a media empire.

I know that Entrepreneurship doesn't start with the letter I. But the 5 I's sound a lot better than 4 I's and an E!

This book will take a look at the 1st I of building wealth which is investing. Beginning to invest can be an extremely daunting task for young and old individuals alike. Determining the proper investment vehicle can be a difficult choice in itself. Choosing where to start amongst stocks, bonds, savings accounts and real estate can be quite bewildering. This book will try to bring clarity to the basic ins and outs of investing.

The 1st Million is the Hardest Million to Make

Why does the 1st million seem so difficult to make? It's the principle of compound interest that makes the 1st million the hardest million that you will ever earn. Here are a few examples.

If you started with $100,000 and would like it to grow to $1,000,000 than you would need a 900% return on your money. ($100,000 + $900,000) = $1,000,000

If you started with $10,000 and would like it to grow to $1,000,000 than you would need a 9,900% return on your money. ($10,000 + $990,000) = $1,000,000

If you started with $1,000 and would like it to grow to $1,000,000 than you would need a 99,900% return on your money. ($1,000 + $999,000) = $1,000,000

If you started with $100 and would like it to grow to

$1,000,000 than you would need a 999,900% return on your money. ($100 + $999,900) = $1,000,000

As you can see it takes astronomical returns on your money to make $100, $1,000, $10,000 and $100,000 grow to a million dollars. Suppose that you already had $1,000,000 dollars and would like to turn it into $2,000,000 dollars. What type of return would you need to achieve that?

($1,000,000 x 100% = $1,000,000) You would need a 100 percent return in order to turn $1,000,000 into $2,000,000 dollars. A 100% return seems paltry compared to the returns listed above. So, what does all of this illustrate? This explains why it is easier for a millionaire to become a multimillionaire than for an individual with a few thousand dollars to become a millionaire. Remember it's not impossible to become a millionaire just remember 2 simple rules.

1. You need to continually increase the amount that you are investing. The greater the amount that you are willing to invest can help lower the return needed to achieve your goals. Saving more money today means that you don't have to chase high returns tomorrow. It's better to be in a position where you can accept a 10% return on your money rather than chasing a 1,000% return.

2. You need to give yourself ample time to reach your financial goal. The principle of compound interest works best for you over longer time periods. All things being equal an individual that invests for 20 years has the potential for a greater return than someone who invests for 5 years.

Chapter 2:

Understanding Savings and Money Market Accounts

Before you begin investing, it is very important to have a savings account to meet any emergency expenses that arise so that you do not have to reach into your investment portfolio. Savings accounts are useful because they are liquid and can meet any emergency cash management needs. The first step to financial freedom is to pick a profitable savings account. All savings accounts are not the same. It is important to pick the savings account with the best interest rate for your money as well as no fees. Bank service fees and account maintenance fees can quickly eat away at any interest earned. Savings accounts can typically be opened with as little as $25.00. Investors with $1,000 or more may wish to consider a money market account. They tend to offer a higher rate of return on a deposit due to the higher balance requirement.

Commercial Bank Savings Accounts: The Worst Savings Accounts

What's the worst deal for your money? These days a savings account at a commercial bank is one of the poorest long term investments for your money. Commercial saving accounts yield some of the lowest rates of return for your money. The national bank average for a traditional savings account is a paltry 0.26%. Check out the rates from some of the country's biggest banks.

A Bank of America regular savings account pays only 0.10% interest rate for your savings. Most savings accounts allow you six free withdrawals per month before being charged a fee. Bank of America only allows 3 withdrawals per month and charges $3 per withdrawal. This is one of the biggest rip-offs going.

Think you could do better with a JPMorgan Chase account? A Chase Bank savings account pays 0.05%. This is the worst return of any savings account that I have found. How about Wells Fargo? A Wells Fargo goal savings account pays the same crummy 0.05%. If you invested $1,000 in a Chase or Wells savings account you would make 50 cents the whole year. You could try US Bank. A US Bank standard savings Account pays just 0.10%. What about Wachovia? Open a Wachovia premium savings account and get 0.05% interest.

A commercial bank savings account is a great way to build wealth **for the bank**. The customer gets paid a terrible interest rate while banks wait and hope that your account drops below the minimum balance so that they can charge you a $3 or $4 dollar monthly fee. Let's say you put $1,000 in a Bank of America savings account and kept it there for one year, you would earn $1.00 on your money. If you let your account drop below $300 for one day, Bank of America will charge you $3.00. It takes all year to earn $1.00 but just one day to lose $3.00.

The days are gone when commercial banks existed to make money for the customer. Banks are in business to maximize their profits. They generate this money by charging customers fees on checking and saving accounts. Remember banks are not stupid. They hire MBA's to figure out the best way to maximize profitability. If your bank is paying you 0.20% interest they know that it will take 360 years before your money doubles. Financial institutions bank on the fact that customers will not be around to see their account balances double. If you can wait that long for your money to grow than a commercial savings account is a good investment.

Assume you invested $500 on January 1 in a traditional bank that was paying .10% interest. Your total interest return for the year would be about $.50. If you invested the same $500 in an account paying 2% under the same terms, your total return for the year would be about $10.00. You can see that the return on just $500 is twenty times greater than the traditional bank.

Online Savings Accounts: A Great Place for Your Cash

So, where should you put your savings? The best place for your savings is at your local credit union or a FDIC insured online savings account. Many credit unions offer rates of at least 1%. For every $1 that you earn in interest at US Bank you could earn 10 times that at a credit union and without the costly fees. Online savings accounts are offering between 1% and 2.5% on savings accounts. You could easily earn 25 times the rate that a large bank is paying.

Websites such as Bankrate.com are excellent resources to use when seeking to pick a savings account with the highest interest rates and minimum balance requirements. Online banks tend to pay much higher interest on saving accounts then traditional banks due to lower overhead costs. Most online banks are FDIC insured financial institutions. Check the FDIC's website to make sure that your online bank is insured. Opening an account at an online bank is a snap. All you need is your personal information and an existing bank account. Your initial deposit can either be mailed or transferred from your regular bank account. A few online banks that you can check out are SmartyPig, ING Direct, Capital One Bank and Emigrant Direct. Interest varies monthly but these banks are currently paying 2.01%, 1.10%, 1.20% and 1.15% respectively.

Depending upon your assets, you might also consider a tiered savings account or a money market account. Tiered savings accounts pay higher interest rates for higher account balances. Money Market Accounts (MMA) offer higher interest rates as well and normally offer limited check writing. These accounts are FDIC insured also.

Credit Unions:
The Place for All Your Banking Needs

Are you looking for a place to get the most bang for your buck? Check out your local credit union. Credit union share accounts are similar to traditional savings accounts but pay higher interest than those financial institutions. Compare the interest rate paid on a savings account at your local credit union with the interest paid at your local brick and mortar financial institution. Credit unions pay a much higher interest rate on all deposit accounts (savings, money market, checking) than banks do. Credit unions typically pay anywhere from 4 to 10 times the amount in interest that you would receive from your local bank. Only online banks pay greater interest than credit unions.

    Credit unions offer the same financial products as banks but they are a whole lot cheaper. Most people use their local credit union for car purchases because the rate is normally lower than dealer financing. Credit unions offer car loans with interest rates as low as 4%. Commercial banks are normally a percentage point or two higher than credit unions. Dealer financing is typically higher than both banks and credit unions. Credit unions are not just a great resource for auto loans. They also offer low interest rates on home loans, home equity lines of credit, signature loans and college loans. They can even save you money on your credit card. The average credit union charges 20 percent less interest than a commercial bank! These savings can easily add up to thousands of dollars over a year.

The Importance of Emergency Savings Accounts

    Financial planners often champion the need for an emergency savings account. Emergency savings accounts are designed to keep you from having to rely on credit when unexpected expenses arise like unemployment, home repairs, auto repairs, hospital bills and etc. But are emergency savings accounts really needed? Definitely! Here is an example of when an emergency savings account came in handy for me.

    I am glad that I had an emergency savings account when I had two emergencies occur where I needed some quick cash. My hot water heater in my house broke and needed to be replaced. I called around for an estimate and a 40 gallon heater with installation cost from $800-$1300. I ended up paying $850 which I thought was pretty fair. A week later I had my sump pump break. This was something that I needed to fix immediately because the sump pump keeps excess water from seeping into the basement. Fortunately, I discovered the problem before any water could flood my basement. A new sump pump cost me $475 with installation.

An emergency savings account has continually proved to be a winner for me over the past few years. When something breaks down it is comforting to know that I don't have to go into debt to pay for the repair. I am saving anywhere from 8-14% by not placing these charges on my credit card. An emergency savings account also keeps me from having to sell an asset (stock, mutual fund, and bond) just to cover the emergency expense. Emergency savings are a lifesaver when a crisis occurs. After I have taken money out of my emergency savings and used it then it's time to build my savings back up again.

Remember that saving is essential for meeting both short term and long term goals. You can even designate accounts for different purposes such as saving for a car purchase or a deposit on a home or even for a vacation. The best way to get started saving is first to make a firm commitment to save a certain amount of money each month. Pick an amount that you will be able to stick to each month. For instance, it is not realistic to think that you will save every single free dollar left over from your discretionary income. Discretionary income is the amount of money that is left over after taxes and living expenses (food, rent, utilities, etc).A good rule of thumb is to begin by saving 10% of every dollar that you receive. This principle can even be followed by high school students and college students alike. Automatic deductions to these accounts can ensure that you make regular contributions at the same time each month.

A disciplined approach to saving is key. Therefore do not make any withdrawals from your savings unless absolutely necessary. Do not get an ATM card for this account or checks for a money market account if you are likely to make frequent withdrawals.

Attitudes and habits that are contrary to saving can really hurt your future goals at financial security. Habits such as spending money consistently on new clothes, shoes and jewelry. You would be surprised at how quickly entertainment expenses such as buying movies, music, going out to eat add up. Always having to have the latest car for example can also hinder your ability to save. It makes no sense to have an expensive luxury automobile, if you do not own a home and have significant savings. These types of habits will keep a person debt ridden for years. Too many Americans already live paycheck to paycheck. You have to adopt the perspective of having your money work for you. Whenever you invest, your money is earning interest and working for you. Whenever you are spending, you are working for your money. Always remember that just because you have the money or credit to pay for something does not mean that you can afford it.

Understanding Savings and Money Market Accounts

Chapter 3:

Investing In Certificates of Deposit & Bonds

A Certificate of Deposit (CD) is a fixed income investment for a specified period of time. This time period is usually from 3 months to 5 years. CD's pay higher interest than traditional savings account. The longer the time period you invest, the higher the interest rate. The only negative drawback to the certificate of deposit is that you can not access your money for the entire term without penalty. Therefore a CD's liquidity is not as great as a savings account. A popular method of investing is CD laddering. This approach allows you to have a CD that is maturing every year while still allowing the individual investor to take advantage of longer term interest rates. An example of this would be buying the following:

If you invested $1500 in the following 3 CD's with the corresponding interest rates.

Term	Interest Rate	Amount
1 year CD	3.75%	$500
2 year CD	4.00%	$500
3 year CD	4.10%	$500

The 1 year CD would mature this year at a 3.75% interest rate. The 2 year CD would mature the following year and the 3 year CD the year after. The investor can either redeem the CD at maturity or allow it to roll over. A CD ladder lets you stay liquid while maximizing the return on your investment dollars.

Many banks today are offering "step up" CD's to entice customers to buy CD's. A "step up" CD gives the owner the right to opt out of their old interest rate and opt in to a higher interest rate. For example, say you invested in a 3 year CD paying 2% interest and a year later the CD rate increased to 3%. Just notify your bank that you want to "step up" to the new rate and you will start earning 3%. It's as simple as that! Here are a few companies offering "step up" CD's. First Midwest Bank has a Rising Rate CD that automatically increases your interest rate every 8 months. Bank of America offers an Opt-Up CD that lets your increase your interest rate during the term of the CD. Ally Bank offers a Raise Your Rate CD which allows you the flexibility of changing your rate one time over the 2 year term.

Types of Savings Bonds: EE, I, HH Bonds

Another option for the investor seeking to preserve capital and generate income is to buy a savings bond. Savings Bonds are Treasury Securities that are guaranteed by the United States Government. Savings Bonds are currently sold in 3 denominations EE bonds, HH bonds and I bonds. EE bonds are issued at 50% of the face value of the bonds. ($50 bond costs $25). Interest is compounded semiannually and the bonds earn interest for 30 years. The EE bonds rate is based upon the 10 year Treasury note and is locked in for the life of the bonds. The current interest rate on EE bonds is 1.20%. The rate is changed on May 1 and November 1 of each year. The bonds can be cashed in anytime after 12 months. However, if you cash the EE bonds in before 5 years then you forfeit the last 3 months interest. EE bonds are an attractive investment when interest rates are high but unattractive when long term interest rates are low.

I bonds are inflation indexed bonds. I bonds are issued at the face value of the bonds. Interest is compounded semiannually and the bonds earn interest for 30 years same as the EE bonds. The I bonds interest rate is based on the fixed rate and the inflation rate. The fixed rate stays the same for the life of the bonds. The inflation rate changes twice a year. The current I bonds interest rate is 3.36% and changes on May 1st and November 1st. The bonds can be cashed in anytime after 12 months. But if you cash them in before 5 years, you lose 3 months worth of interest. I bonds are an excellent investment during times of rising inflation.

HH bonds are current income securities that earn interest every six months. Unlike EE and I bonds which pay interest when they are cashed in, HH bonds deposit the interest in your account twice a year. The current rate of interest on HH bonds is 1.50%. The minimum amount that you can buy HH bonds for is $500.00. The bonds can be held for 20 years and still earn interest. HH bonds can only be purchased by trading in EE bonds for them.

T-bills and Treasury Bonds

T-bills are short term securities that mature in less than 1 year. You can buy a 4 week, 13 week, 26 week or 52 week bill. T-bills don't pay interest but are sold at a discount to their face value. The face value of a Treasury bill is $1,000. T-bills are bought via an auction process. For example, let's say you bought a $1,000 Treasury bill at a price of $950, than you would receive the full $1,000 when you redeem the bond. You would have earned $50 in interest giving you an effective yield of 5.2%. You can buy a T-bill through your local bank, broker or the TreasuryDirect website.

Treasury bonds are the exact opposites of T-bills. Treasury bonds are long term securities that have a maturity date of 30 years. They pay interest every six months and are sold in lots of $100 dollars. Treasury bonds are great for locking in a high rate of interest for an extended time period. You can currently purchase a 30 year treasury bond yielding almost 5%.

Corporate Bonds

One type of bond that investors tend to be less familiar with are corporate bonds. Corporate bonds are debt securities that are issued by a company. Corporate bonds can be purchased in blocks of $1,000. Corporate bonds pay interest semiannually. The maturity date of corporate bonds may vary from 1 year to 30 years. Corporate bonds are priced and listed on major exchanges. Bond prices rise as market interest rates fall and bond prices fall as interest rates rise.

If you purchased a 10 year bond for $1,000 with an 8 percent interest rate and want to sell it after 4 years when interest is at 6 percent, you would be able to sell the bond at a premium because it is paying more interest than new bonds. Buying a bond at a premium will cost you more than the par value of $1,000. Buying a bond at a discount means that you are paying under $1,000.

Corporate bonds have greater risk than savings bonds because the bonds are backed by the individual company. Therefore the interest rates offered on corporate bonds are much greater than government backed bonds. Corporate bonds are rated based upon the financial strength of the company. Bonds are rated by Moody's and Standard and

Poor's. Bonds of the highest quality will receive an AAA rating. Whereas bonds of lower quality will receive a CCC or D rating. Corporate bonds can be purchased through a broker or simply by visiting the company's website.

Municipals and Bond Funds

Municipal bonds are state and local government obligations that are used to fund public projects like bridges, hospitals, and schools. Municipal bonds pay a lower interest rate than corporate bonds but are exempt from state and local taxes.

Another way to buy bonds is through bond funds. Bond funds allow you to diversify among short term, intermediate, and long term bonds. PIMCO, Vanguard, Natixis and T Rowe Price are just a few of the companies that offer popular short term bond funds.

Investing in Certificates of Deposit & Bonds

Chapter 4:

Retirement Accounts

Planning for retirement is one of the most critical endeavors that an individual must undertake. Many people have questions about the different types of retirement accounts available and which one is the right plan for them. Selecting the proper retirement plan can help to ensure a smooth transition into retirement. We will take a look at a few of the more popular retirement plans available: a Roth IRA and a Traditional IRA.

An individual retirement account (IRA) is a personal retirement savings plan for those who receive taxable income during the year. Think of an IRA as an umbrella and you can put almost anything that you want under it. An IRA may be invested in stocks, bonds, mutual funds, certificates of deposits, money markets and real estate. Individual retirement accounts can either be set up with a bank, broker, credit union or a mutual fund.

What is a Roth IRA?

A Roth IRA is an individual retirement account which allows an individual to set aside a specified dollar amount of income after taxes. This tax-advantaged retirement account derives its name from United States Congressman William Victor Ross Jr., who was the legislative sponsor of the bill creating this plan. A Roth IRA provides tax free growth of your money in lieu of getting a tax deduction.

Roth IRA Eligibility

Here are a few of the rules to be eligible to fully contribute to a Roth IRA:

- If you are a single tax filer your modified adjusted gross income needs to be less than $105,000. Married tax filers need their income to be less than $167,000.
- The maximum annual contribution is $5,000 per person. Married couples can contribute $10,000. If you are 50 or older you can contribute $6,000 per person annually due to a catch-up provision.
- Your contributions can be withdrawn at any time and are not tax deductible because they are made in after tax dollars.

Roth IRA's are an easy way of creating tax free income and growth for your retirement portfolio. Let's say you invested $5,000 annually over a 20 year period into a Roth IRA, and at the end of 20 years, your money grew to $500,000. You may have lost out on the tax deduction on the $100,000, but you do not have to pay any taxes on the $500,000 when you withdraw funds after age 59 and a half. This can add up to a substantial savings as your earnings increase.

Roth IRA Advantages

Tax Free Growth – Earnings are not subject to income tax as long as you have held the account for at least 5 years, and you are at least 59 1/2.

Easy Withdrawal Process – Direct contributions can be withdrawn at any time, tax free.

Multiple Retirement Accounts – A Roth IRA can be set up even if you have another retirement plan.

No minimum withdrawal requirements – There are no required minimum distributions as in a traditional IRA or 401(k).

Inheritance – Assets can be passed onto beneficiaries after death.

Roth IRA Restrictions

No Tax Deductions – Contributions are not tax deductible as they are in Traditional IRA's and 401(k)'s.

Income limits on participation- You may not be eligible to enroll in a Roth IRA if your income is higher than the income limits.

Early Withdrawal Fees – There is a 10% early withdrawal fee if you withdraw money before 59 1/2 without a qualified reason (education expenses, first time home purchase, disability, medical expenses, death, health insurance, etc).

What is a Traditional IRA?

A traditional IRA is an individual retirement account which allows an individual to set aside a specified dollar amount of income and to obtain a tax deduction for these contributions. A traditional IRA allows all earnings to grow tax deferred. The main advantage of a traditional IRA is the tax deduction on contributions. These tax deductions reduce the tax liability of the contributor.

Traditional IRA Eligibility

Here are the rules to be eligible to fully contribute to a Traditional IRA:

- All United States taxpayers that are not active participants in an employer sponsored plan are eligible to make contributions to a Traditional IRA plan.
- The maximum annual contribution is $5,000 per person. Married couples can contribute $10,000. If you are 50 or older you can contribute $6,000 per person annually due to a catch-up provision.
- Your contributions are tax deductible up to 100%.

Traditional IRA's are a great way to save money and get a tax deduction at the same time. If you invest $5,000 annually into a Traditional IRA, you can claim a $5,000 tax deduction. This tax deduction will lower your adjusted gross income which lowers your tax liability. You do not have to pay any taxes on your contributions until you withdraw funds or at the age of 70 ½.

Traditional IRA Advantages

Tax Deductions – All contributions are fully tax deductible as long as your employer doesn't offer a qualified retirement plan. If you are covered by an employer's plan than you may still be eligible to receive a tax deduction depending upon your filing status and if you fall within certain income thresholds. Single filers that participate in their company's retirement plan and earn $56,000 or less are eligible for a full deduction. Married filers that are active participants in their company's plan and earn $89,000 or less are also eligible for a full income tax deduction.

No Income Limits On Participation- Everyone is eligible to enroll in a Traditional IRA but not everyone is eligible to receive a tax deduction.

Lower Tax Liability – Contributions can grow tax deferred and withdrawals can be taken in later years to reduce your tax liability. Since income is often lower during retirement years, funds withdrawn may be subject to lower taxes.

Multiple Retirement Accounts – A Traditional IRA can be set up even if you have another retirement plan. Contributions may not be fully tax deductible if you have enough qualified retirement plan.

Bankruptcy Protection – Contributions are protected from creditors.

Inheritance – You can pass assets onto beneficiaries after death.

Traditional IRA Restrictions

Minimum Withdrawal Requirements - There are required minimum distributions unlike in a Roth IRA. Withdrawals must begin at age 70 ½. If you fail to withdraw your required minimum distribution, the amount not withdrawn is taxed by the government at 50%.

Safeguarding Your 401(k)

During this time of economic uncertainty in the United States economy there have been major declines in the U.S. housing and financial markets. Many individuals are concerned about their financial well being. This is a good time to evaluate your overall financial condition and safeguard your finances. One of the best places to start is by looking at your 401(k).

A 401(k) is an employer sponsored retirement plan that allows employees to receive a tax deduction on contributions. Distributions are subject to taxes upon withdrawal. One of the best parts about a 401(k) plan is that employers can offer matching contributions to employee plans. These matching contributions are free money that is given to employees. 401(k) product offerings are determined by your employer. They provide a group of financial products and the employees have to choose from these offerings.

This is a great time to evaluate your risk exposure in your 401(k). According to the Financial Industry Regulatory Authority, "One-third of employees eligible to invest in company stock through their 401(k) have more than 20% in their company's stock"[1]. Are you overly concentrated in any particular asset class? Does your portfolio contain more than 20 percent of your own company stock? There are valuable lessons that can be learned from the Enron bankruptcy, Lehman Brothers crisis, Washington Mutual insolvency and the Bear Stearns failure. A large number of the employees of these firms lost their jobs and their life savings by placing all of their eggs in one basket.

A good rule of thumb to follow is to never invest greater than 20 percent of your money in your own company's individual stock. You don't want to lose both your job and

---

1   Motley Fool. "A Bear Market For 401(k) Plans"

retirement savings just because you placed too much trust in your company. Your only defense is diversification. Your 401(k) should contain a mixture of stock mutual funds, bonds mutual funds and cash to truly be considered diversified. Bond income and interest earned on cash savings can help generate positive returns when equity prices are declining.

Retirement Accounts

Chapter 5:

Introduction to Stocks

Once you have established an effective savings strategy, you may wish to invest in the stock market. In this chapter, we will discuss the benefits of investing in stock, the risk versus rewards of investing in stock and how to properly evaluate a stock. This chapter should help in formulating a basic understanding of investing in equities.

Benefits of Owning Stock

What is a stock exactly? A simple definition of stock would be ownership in a company. Each share of stock that you own represents a fractional share of ownership in the company. As a shareholder of a company, you possess a number of rights:

(1) the right to vote on major corporate issues.

(2) the right to share in the profits paid out by the company.

(3) the right to attend shareholder meetings.

Shareholders should take an active role in participating in proxy voting, reading all company financial reports and listening to quarterly conference calls. They have the right to vote on topics such as management, changes in

Introduction to Stocks

company policy and executive compensation. Shareholders are also entitled to any dividends that have been paid out by the company based on their percentage of stock ownership. Shareholders also get to attend shareholder meetings that typically take place annually at the corporate headquarters.

Stocks offer the opportunity for much greater returns than savings accounts. The stock market has historically returned an average annual rate greater then 10%. This return is greater than real estate, treasury bonds, gold, certificates of deposit and savings accounts. There is an excellent article, by Dr. Jeremy Siegel called Stocks the Asset of Choice for the Long Run, which explains that for long term investing no other asset class has delivered the return of the stock market.

Risks in Owning Stock

However, stocks also carry much greater risks than other asset classes. All stocks are subject to systematic risk. Systematic risk is risk that can not be diversified away because it is inherent in the market itself. Market risk is the risk that an investment will decrease due to a general market decline. Company specific risk is the risk inherent in a company and that the stock price can decline and remain downward for an extended period of time. There are other types of risk such as political, country specific and foreign exchange rate risk that may apply to foreign investments.

Unsystematic risk is the risk that lies within a specific investment. This type of risk can be diversified away through proper asset allocation. The risk of an investment is directly correlated to the return of an investment. Savings accounts and C/D's have little to no risk and thus offer a very modest return. It is important to consider your risk tolerance before investing in any security. Warren Buffett teaches that investors should be able to weather significant market declines up to as much as 50 percent without becoming paralyzed by fear. You should avoid investing in the stock market if the thought of possible losses terrifies you.

How to Value a Stock

Stocks are valued based upon a combination of factors such as price to earnings ratio (P/E), earnings per share, market cap, net income, profitability, debt/equity ratio, cash flows, return on assets, and return on equity.

Price to Earnings Ratio

Typically the higher the projected sales growth, the higher a company's price to earnings ratio (P/E). The P/E ratio is the price of a stock divided by it's earnings per share.

$$P/E = \frac{\text{Price of Stock}}{\text{Earnings per Share}}$$

The P/E ratio can help in determining how expensive a stock is currently. The price to earnings ratio helps to identify how much is being paid for each dollar of earnings. A stock with a P/E ratio of 25 shows that an investor is willing to pay $25 for every $1 of earnings. The higher the P/E ratio, the more expensive a stock tends to be. When investing it is important to remember that the P/E ratio is a good starting point to determine a company's value. A company's P/E ratio should be compared to its growth rate. If a company is growing at 20% and has a P/E of 18, this company may be a bargain. Conversely if a company is growing at 20% and has

Introduction to Stocks

a P/E of 50, this company may be considered expensive. A good rule of thumb to follow is to never buy a stock whose P/E ratio is more than twice the company's growth rate.

A company's P/E ratio should also be compared to the industry average. Price to earnings ratios of competitors can be useful in deciding if a company is selling at a discount or a premium to its rivals. It is important not to compare ratios of companies in different sectors. For example, Consolidated Edison has a P/E of 17 and Apple Inc. 34. These two companies operate in different industries which makes the P/E ratios drastically different. Energy companies normally have low P/E's whereas technology companies have much higher multiples. Never compare P/E ratios of two companies in different industries.

Earnings per Share

The most important factor in most companies' stock price valuation is earnings. Earnings expectations have a direct correlation to stock price. The higher the earnings growth expected, the more expensive the stock's P/E. The earnings of a company are reflected in the earnings per share.

EPS = <u>Net Income – Dividends paid to preferred stockholders</u>
Weighted Average Number of Shares Outstanding

Earnings per share is the amount of a company's profit allocated to each share of stock. This is a critical metric to use in determining a share price. In any investment decision, look at trailing earnings per share (past years EPS), current earnings per share (this year's EPS) and forward earnings per share (projected EPS). A declining EPS is a strong signal of declining income and decreasing sales. Further investigation may reveal that this is just a temporary setback or a permanent crisis.

Market Capitalization: Small Cap, Mid Cap, Large Cap

The market capitalization, known as the market cap, is a measure that is useful for determining the total value of a business. This is the current market value of the entire company. It is expressed in the following equation.

Market Cap = Stock Price x Number of Shares Outstanding

Market cap can be useful in determining the level of risk associated with an investment and the return that should be expected. Micro cap companies are the most volatile. These are very small companies with very little assets and therefore not much financial protection. These companies may have the potential for great growth and could become the next Microsoft. Conversely, they have the least downside protection and could become the next Etoys. Etoys was an online retailer that went bankrupt when the dot-com bubble burst. Small cap companies are subject to wild price swings also. They are small companies that may have growth potential but are quite risky. Small caps are relatively young in the growth cycle. Mid cap companies offer less growth potential but more stability than micro and small caps. They tend to have better financial statements which is why they have more assets and revenue. Their stock price fluctuations are not as volatile as small caps and micro small caps. Large cap companies are well established companies that typically have the least growth potential but the greatest financial security. These companies typically pay dividends to shareholders and tend to be the most stable stocks. The smaller the market cap, the greater the risk. Therefore the potential reward must be greater to take on the added risk.

Market Capitalization Categories

Micro Cap Stocks have market caps of $250 million or less.

Small Cap Stocks have market caps from $250 million to $1 billion.

Mid Cap Stocks have market caps from $1 billion to $10 billion.

Large Cap Stocks have market caps from $10 billion and up.

Dividend Yield

Another important measure in considering a stock investment is the dividend yield. The dividend yield shows exactly how much a company has paid out annually in dividends in relation to the share price. This yield is shown as a percentage.

$$\text{Dividend Yield} = \frac{\text{Dividend per share}}{\text{Price per Share}}$$

Dividends are the distributions of company earnings that are given to shareholders. It is important to note that not all stocks pay dividends. Young companies that are still in the growth stage typically do not pay dividends. The earnings are normally reinvested in the company to further future growth and expansion. Mature companies that are profitable normally pay dividends. Dividends may be paid in the form of cash or stock. Dividends are paid out to shareholders on a quarterly basis. Shareholders may choose to have cash dividends reinvested to purchase more shares. Dividends are important because they are the only real return that investors receive on a stock until shares are sold.

Debt to Equity

The debt/equity ratio, will help you determine exactly how leveraged a firm is. The debt/equity ratio is calculated in the following equation.

$$\text{Debt/Equity Ratio} = \frac{\text{Total Liabilities}}{\text{Shareholders' Equity}}$$

The lower the debt to equity ratio, the less a company is financing its growth with debt. A debt to equity ratio below 0.5 is considered excellent. A debt/equity ratio over 1 may be a cause for concern as the company is likely financing assets with debt. Always compare debt ratios with firms in the same industries. Technology companies have the best balance sheets and will therefore have very low debt to equity ratios. Manufacturing companies rely heavily on debt and will have a much higher ratio. Invest in firms with debt levels lower than competitors because heavily leveraged firms have a far greater risk of bankruptcy.

Return on Equity & Return on Assets

If you want to judge the managerial skills of the executive team, take a look at the Return on Equity (ROE) and Return on Assets (ROA). Return on assets and return on equity will give you a better understanding of how effectively the management team is utilizing company resources. The two equations can be found below.

$$\text{ROA} = \frac{\text{Net Income}}{\text{Total Assets}} \qquad \text{ROE} = \frac{\text{Net Income}}{\text{Total Equity}}$$

Return on equity will give you insight into how the company is managing its investment dollars. This is also commonly referred to as Return on Net Worth. ROE demonstrates the effectiveness of company management. Meanwhile ROA tells you how efficiently management is deploying its assets. Search for companies with an above average ROE and ROA. A good reference point is to look for companies that have delivered double digit returns in both categories for a minimum of 5 years. Companies that consistently outperform the industry average have a management team that is doing things the right way.

The Balance Sheet, Income Statement, Cash Flow Statement

If you want to judge the health of any company, take a look at the balance sheet, income statement, and cash flow statement. The balance sheet will show you the financial health of the company. A balance sheet lists all of the company's asset's, liabilities, and owners' equity. You can find everything that a company owns and owes right on the balance sheet. Look for companies with twice as many assets as liabilities and that have very little debt. The income statement is known as the profit and loss statement. All of a company's revenue and expenses are listed on the income statement. The income statement will help you assess how profitable a firm has been over the past year. Profitable firms have net income and unprofitable ones have net losses. Look for companies with five years of revenue growth and five years of increasing earnings per share. The cash flow statement tells you how a company is spending its cash. The cash flow statement documents inflows and outflows of cash for the year. Avoid companies with high cash burn rates. These are companies that have more outflows than inflows. Companies with more inflows than outflows can accumulate huge war chests.

    Other important data that is useful when researching stocks are the earnings growth rate, sales growth rate, and net income. The earnings growth rate shows you how rapidly a firm is increasing earnings.

10 Things to Look for When Buying a Stock

Learn from the master. The world's greatest investor, Warren Buffett invests in stocks that have the following characteristics:

1. Wide Economic Moat – major competitive advantage.

2. Easy to Understand Business - easy to understand how they make their money.

3. Return on Equity - measures how fast a company can grow earnings (15% minimum).

4. High Profit Margins - profit margins higher than industry peers.

5. Consistent Operating Results - profit to sales ratio less than 2, price to cash flow under 12.

6. Long Term Earnings Growth - favorable long term prospects for growth (5 consecutive years of growth).

7. Strong Management Team - honest management focused on creating value for shareholders.

8. Low Debt - debt to equity ratio lower than .30.

9. Margin of Safety - selling at a discount to true value (selling at less than 1.5 times book value).

10. Consistent Operating Performance - minimum of 5 years consistent operating results.

Introduction to Stocks

Chapter 6:

The Art of Investing

Buying My First Stock

I remember buying my first stock after I had graduated from college. I had bought my first mutual fund at 19 and was now ready to dabble in the stock market. I had just gotten my degree in finance and was sure that I knew everything about investing. So I sat down and picked my first investment.

The first stock that I ever bought was Krispy Kreme Doughnuts. I just knew that Krispy Kreme Doughnuts was a great investment. I was sure of it. Krispy Kreme was rapidly opening new stores and was making tons of money. Why was I so sure? Because of their financial statements? Nope, never even looked at them. Because of their competitive advantage? Nope, no clue what that was. I bought $2,000 worth of Krispy Kreme stock because of the long lines that I would see whenever the "Hot Doughnuts Now" sign lit up. My investment thesis was lots of people equals lots of money.

Little did I know but I was wrong. Krispy Kreme was crushed by a poor business model and the low carb diet craze. Krispy Kreme was only making money by constantly opening new stores. Their same store stores sales were terrible.

The excitement for hot doughnuts quickly went away once a Krispy Kreme store was open for awhile. People shunned its fattening products for low carb alternatives. Their parking lots were soon empty and a lot of the stores have closed up. My "wise" analysis quickly turned my $2,000 into $1,400.

So, what can you learn from my story. Always do your homework. Never invest in something just because you see a lot of people there. Have you ever had someone tell you, Invest in ABC company because you know they are making money? The assumption is that crowded stores mean massive profits. Never invest based on random assumptions. Invest based on the fundamentals. If not, then you just may end up owning the next Krispy Kreme Doughnuts.

Study The Masters

In developing a strategy for investing it is wise to look at the investment styles of successful investors such as Warren Buffett and Benjamin Graham. These men adopted long term approaches to purchasing undervalued stocks. Buffett invests based upon Benjamin Graham's approach to value investing. Graham believed that the fair value of a stock is based on its future earnings power. The key therefore to investing is to purchase wonderful companies at fair prices. Value investing involves buying companies with wide economic moats that are selling at a discount to their intrinsic value. Value investors look to buy stocks that are undervalued and then hold these stocks until the rest of the market realizes the real value of the company's assets. These companies may have been beaten down in price because of some negative event or may be in an industry that is simply overlooked by investors. An example of an overlooked industry is waste management and disposal. This industry would tend to be overlooked by most investors because it does not have the flashy appeal of an industry such as computer software. Below is an example of a solid company in a boring industry that just generates profits.

Case Study: Waste Management

According to Peter Lynch, famed author of One Up on Wall Street, sometimes you can find profitable companies in overlooked industries. The garbage industry contains a company that I would consider a Lynch type investment opportunity.

Waste Management (WMI) is the market leader in trash collection, disposal and recycling services in the US. The company operates in an industry with a high barrier to entry as the garbage industry is extremely capital intensive. Waste Management provides a service that has been needed in the past and will continue to be needed for the foreseeable future. The company's stock currently trades at $28.60 per share which is relatively cheap based on it PE of 14 which is well below the industry average. Waste Management has a forward PE of 13 per share based on 2010 expected earnings which are just below $2.20 per share. The company has done an admirable job of achieving strong stable earnings growth historically.

Waste Management has strong pricing power. Even in this recessionary environment the company's prices rose as overall volume declined. EPS and ROE are much higher then industry competitors. Earnings are expected to grow in the double digits over the next 5 years at a rate of

11% per annum. Return on Equity is in the double digits as well at an impressive 17.4%. Waste Management pays a healthy dividend of $1.16 which amounts to a generous 4.1% yield. The company is almost worth buying on the merits of its dividend alone. Companies like Waste Management will not be the hot stock of the day on financial television but this should not stop companies like this from finding a place in your investment portfolio.

Stay Away from "Hot Stock Tips"

Have you ever turned on a cable financial news channel and noticed a network pundit touting the next great investment? CNBC may have an analyst telling you that a small tech company is the next Microsoft and you must buy it today. Fox Business may have a gold expert telling you to buy gold despite the fact that gold is selling at a 30 year high. Or you may be at a social function and someone is talking about an investment that is guaranteed to double over the next year. What is the average investor to do with all of these "hot tips"? My advice to you is **To Tune Out The Noise**.

It can be tempting to try to make a quick killing and buy the hot idea that everyone is talking about. But more often then not you will end up getting burned and regretting that you ever wasted your precious dollars. Take the dot-com bubble of 2000 for example. In the late 90's companies like MicroStrategy, Worldcom and America Online were soaring to new highs daily. The internet was the place to be and everyone was investing in the tech sector. People were quitting their jobs and daytrading stocks full-time in hopes of getting rich. In 2000 the tech bubble burst and many daytraders found themselves declaring bankruptcy.

Another example is the real estate bubble of

2008. During the early 2000's home prices increased dramatically to record levels fueling speculative home buying. Speculators bought homes with little to no money down in hopes of flipping them for a quick profit. Everywhere you looked people were buying homes hoping to flip them and get rich overnight. The housing market was saturated with people bidding home prices up to unsustainable levels. The bottom fell out of the housing bubble in 2007 with the subprime crisis and millions of people found themselves facing foreclosure or bankruptcy.

The lesson to be learned from both cases is to **Never Follow The Crowd**. While there will always be speculators trying to make a fast buck with their get rich quick schemes; remember that real wealth is built over time. Wealth building is a marathon and not a sprint. Building wealth is a long term endeavor that requires having a solid strategy and being committed to it.

3 Simple Steps to Investing for The Long Run

1) Identify your investment strategy.

Your investment strategy shapes the selection of your investment portfolio. Your investment strategy depends on a number of factors such as your age, risk tolerance and investment horizon. If your strategy is to secure a guaranteed return so that you can sleep at night then your portfolio may consist of conservative low risk assets such as Treasury bonds, savings bonds and certificates of deposits. If you are a high risk investor that seeks a greater return on your money then your portfolio may consist of individual stocks, small cap mutual funds, and high yielding bonds.

2) Invest in undervalued assets.

The key to investing is to find an undervalued asset and to hold it until the intrinsic value is realized. The intrinsic value is the true value of the asset. When investing you want to find an asset whose intrinsic value is greater than the current market value. Once the intrinsic value is equal to or greater than the market value, you sell. The asset can be anything of monetary value including stocks, bonds, mutual funds, real estate, etc. For example let's say that you wanted to buy 1 share of McDonald's with a market value of $50. If you believe that the true value of McDonald's is $70 then you would hold the stock until McDonald's reaches its intrinsic value.

3) Ignore short term market fluctuations.

Financial networks are only concerned with the short term outlook. The day to day movements of the market should only concern speculators. Only invest if your minimum investment time frame is a minimum of 5 years. If your investment reaches its intrinsic value in less than that time period, that's great! If not, don't worry. Be patient! You are investing for the long run.

Chapter 7:

Shaping Your Investment Strategy

Step 1:
Developing your overall investment objectives.

An important step that any individual should take in investing is to clearly define and develop one's investment objectives. Determining your investment goals and objectives will help you in finding the best strategies to meet your goals. There are some key questions listed below that can help you in formulating your investment strategy. Grab a pen and paper and write down the answers to the following questions.

What purpose are you investing for?

This is the most important question because it pertains to your investment purpose. The purpose of your investment could range from retirement needs, children's education, purchasing a home, buying an automobile or simply financial independence. Setting goals helps to add a clear cut direction to your investment strategy. If you have a specific purpose in mind, then you will be much more likely to stick to your plan.

What is the exact amount of money that you will need?

Now you have to figure out the amount of money needed to reach this goal. Your goal may be as small as $5,000 or as large as $20 million dollars. Write this amount down so that you know what you are aiming for. Listing the amount of money needed will help you in figuring the necessary weekly or monthly contributions necessary to accomplish your goal.

When will you need access to the money?

Next, it is important to determine your time frame. The time frame may range from as short as a few months to 50 years. Determining the time frame for cash needs is critical in ensuring selection of the proper investment vehicle and proper scheduling of the necessary distributions. For example, if you invested $10,000 in a 5 year certificate of deposit and wanted to withdraw the cash after 3 years, you would not be able to access the cash without paying a substantial penalty.

How much of a return do you expect on your money?

So, exactly what kind of return are you looking for on your investment? Be reasonable! Don't expect returns of 50 or 100 percent yearly. Even the greatest investors find it difficult to beat the market year after year. The average return of the market is 10 percent annually historically. The return on your investment should directly relate to the amount of risk that you are willing to take.

How much risk are you willing to take?

Figuring out your risk tolerance will be useful in determining the securities that best fit your particular needs. If seeing your portfolio lose 30 or 40 percent of its value causes you nightmares, then you may want to stick to guaranteed investments such as C/D's and Treasury bills.

Are you willing to sacrifice in order to meet this goal?

Eliminating unnecessary expenses and purchases can make the difference in realizing your dreams. You have to know the difference between a want and a need. A need is something that is essential, whereas a want is a luxury. In order to accomplish your long term goals, you may have to sacrifice some short term wants.

Needs	**Wants**
Owning a Home	$500,000 Home
Car	Luxury Automobile
Clothes	New Outfit Every Weekend

Step 2:
Figuring out your asset allocation.

Once you have written down your investment objectives, you are now ready to begin asset allocation. Many financial planners will tell you that asset allocation is the single most important factor in building a portfolio. Asset allocation is the process of dividing an investment portfolio among asset classes. The three major asset classes are stocks, bonds and cash. However, these are not the only asset classes. Other asset classes that exist are real estate, private equity, natural resources, foreign currencies and derivatives.

The objective of asset allocation is to provide diversification for your portfolio. Proper asset allocation involves a number of factors. Your assets should be allocated according to your age, risk tolerance, and investment horizon. Typically, the younger the individual the larger the percentage of money that should be invested in equities. For example, a person in their 20's may devote over 80% of their portfolio to stocks, whereas a retiree may have less than 20% of their overall portfolio in stocks. The longer the time period that you have to invest, the larger the growth you should expect in your portfolio.

Risk tolerance refers to the degree of risk you are willing to accept in return for potentially higher returns. Aggressive investors are more willing to accept significant fluctuations in value in exchange for the possibility of greater rates of return. The potential return must be high enough to make it worth the potential loss of investment capital. Capital appreciation is the primary goal of aggressive investors. Conservative investors are less willing to accept these fluctuations. Capital preservation is the main priority of conservative investors. Understanding your ability to handle risk can help to save you from sleepless nights and second guessing of your decisions.

Investment horizon is the length of time that you invest before you begin to use the money. For example, an individual that will need to use the money invested in 10 years, has an investment horizon of 10 years. A good rule of thumb is, the longer the investment horizon, the more aggressive that you can be as an investor. This is because long term investors have the ability to ride out short term market downturns among asset classes. Remember that investors in stocks should have a minimum investment horizon of 5 years.

Step 3:
Selecting the proper security.

Numbers of people invest in retirement plans with no idea exactly what assets they have in their plans. They purchase mutual funds without knowing what particular securities the fund is purchasing. You need to know what type of investor you are to make sure that you pick a suitable investment for your needs. Are you a passive investor or an active investor? Let's take a look at passive investing vs. active investing.

Passive Investing

Passive investing is often great for the beginning investor because it provides broad diversification with minimal costs. Passive investing is an investment strategy in which an individual makes as few transactions as possible. Buying and selling transactions are limited in order to minimize transaction costs and capital gains taxes. Passive investors follow a buy and hold approach when it comes to investing. They are seeking long term capital appreciation with limited activity. Passive investing can be used for just about any asset class including stocks, bonds, real estate, and commodities. Passive investing is favored for its low turnover, diversification, less decision making, and lower taxes. The disadvantages of passive investing are that index funds can never outperform the market and are subject to tracking error.

Index Funds:
The Passive Investor's Best Friend

One of the most popular passive investments is an index fund. An index fund is a mutual fund that is designed to track the movements of a specific financial market by proportionally holding every security in a given market. For example, let's say you were to purchase the Vanguard S&P 500 index fund (I picked this fund because it is one of the largest index funds in the world). You would be buying a fund whose performance would replicate the performance of the S&P 500. If the S&P 500 increased 10% during 2010, then the Vanguard S&P 500 Index Fund should be up approximately 10% as well. As you can see from this example, index funds aim to duplicate the performance of a given market.

Index Exchange Traded Funds:
A New Way to Passively Invest

Another way to passively invest is through an Index Exchange Traded Fund (ETF). Index exchange traded funds have been growing in popularity since the 90's. They allow you to track an index like a traditional index fund but the price changes throughout the day just like a stock. Index ETFs can be purchased and sold anytime during market hours. Index mutual funds calculate their share prices at the end of the day so they can only be bought and sold after the market closes. The advantages of an index ETF are that the expense ratios and taxable distributions are typically lower than index mutual funds.

Active Investing

Active investing is an investment strategy where the individual investor is more involved in the buying and selling of securities. Active investors believe that by managing their own money they can beat the return of the stock market. The advantages of active investing are that it allows investors to quickly take advantage of undervalued market sectors, provides the potential for greater profits and returns than the overall market and index funds, and provides greater control over an investment. The disadvantages of active investing are that active investors have much higher management fees and expenses than other investments, can provide more taxable income, leaving you subject to more taxes, and can underperform the market due to poor investment strategies.

Mutual Funds

The most popular investment for active investors is a mutual fund. The majority of funds sold by mutual fund companies are actively managed. Most retirement accounts and brokerage accounts are comprised of actively managed mutual funds. An actively managed fund is a fund where a manager regularly buys and sells investments. The active investor aims to outperform a specific stock market index such as the S&P 500 or the Dow Jones. A fund manager in an actively managed fund may re-balance the fund as frequently as once a quarter. Active investors believe that the stock market is inefficient and that they are able to benefit from its inefficiencies by purchasing securities when they are undervalued.

For example, if you purchased a value fund. This fund would typically purchase out-of-favor stocks from different sectors that the fund manager believes are selling at a discount. Value fund managers like Bruce Berkowitz have found great success investing in highly distressed assets. Berkowitz has consistently outperformed the S&P 500 index over the last 10 years.

Look for mutual funds with low expense ratios. Pick a mutual fund with an expense ratio of 1% or lower. Stay away from funds with 12b-1 fees, front loaded fees, back loaded fees, and high annual expenses. Avoid investing in hot funds that have been on a tear for a few years. These funds typically attract a lot of new investor money which makes it hard for the fund manager to duplicate past results. Funds like Fidelity Magellan were great investments for early investors but its performance has lagged the market in recent years. As funds swell with assets, it becomes more difficult for fund managers to invest in smaller companies with growth potential. Find a mutual fund with $5 billion or less in assets from a reputable fund company with a low expense ratio and a great management team.

Stock Investing

Individual stocks are another popular investment vehicle for active investors. One of the biggest proponents of an active investing strategy is Jim Cramer. Cramer's philosophy is that the active investor should take control of their future by abandoning passive investments. Passive investors have a buy and hold strategy; active investors have a "buy and do homework" strategy. It's called a buy and do homework strategy because active investors have to research their investments by reading and analyzing financial statements. Surprisingly enough, Warren Buffett is an active investor himself! That's right, Buffett researches and actively invests in companies that he believes represent a compelling value. It's important to remember that Buffett is an active investor not an active trader. Congratulations! Once you have answered these questions you have created your investment purpose.

Shaping Your Investment Strategy

Chapter 8:

Getting Started Investing

Last year Fox Business aired a television special about Warren Buffett called Buffett U. Warren Buffett hosted a question and answer session with business school students from all over the country. The students were allowed to ask Buffett questions about any topic that they wished. I found one of Buffett's comments particularly interesting.

Buffett explained his investment philosophy as a young investor. He stated that he always believed in investing in great companies at discounted prices. But he was a much more active investor when he was younger. Buffett explained that he began with only $9,800 so he would have to sell one investment in order to purchase a better investment. If he had invested in a company selling for 80 cents on the dollar then he would sell his investment to purchase a company trading at 60 cents on a dollar.

This is intriguing because this differs from the buy and hold forever Buffett of the latter years. I am not trying to suggest that Warren Buffett was daytrading stocks! But he was selling cheap stocks to purchase cheaper stocks. I think that this illustrates that when you are investing small amounts of capital, you have to always seek the greatest return on capital. This may mean selling a good

Getting Started Investing

investment idea for a great one.

For example, let's say you had about $23,000 to invest. You bought 1000 shares of American Express (AXP) at $23 per share because you believe that AXP has an intrinsic value of $30 per share. This equates to a $7 per share potential gain and a 30% profit. A few months later when American Express is trading at $25, you notice that Best Buy is selling at $20 per share. You believe however that Best Buy has an intrinsic value of $35 per share. This represents a $15 per share gain and a 75% profit. You can see that the most profitable move is to buy Best Buy despite the fact that you didn't receive the full value for American Express.

Buffett is now rich enough that he no longer needs to sell one opportunity to recognize another. If you are not quite as rich as Buffett (like me) and want to maximize returns with less money then consider these tips. Always set an intrinsic value for an investment and aim to realize that value. Be flexible. If a more attractive opportunity presents itself then adapt your investment strategy.

5 Ways to Start Investing with $50

It doesn't take $9,800 for you to get started investing. You can invest with as little as $50. That's right! You can buy stock with as little as $50.

1) The first step is to determine what asset class that you would like to invest in. You can invest in any asset class (stocks, bonds, mutual funds, CD's) online.

2) Now it's time to get started. If you choose to invest in stock, you can use online sites like Buyandhold or Sharebuilder which allow you to buy stock with only $20. These sites have very low fees and are great for the beginning investor. Buyandhold has a fee of only $6.99 per month which gives you 2 free trades every month. Sharebuilder has no monthly fee and charges just $4 to buy stock and $9.95 to sell stock.

3) If you choose to invest in bonds, you can use the TreasuryDirect website. TreasuryDirect is the US government's official website that sells US savings bonds. I bonds and EE bonds can be bought for as little as $25.

4) If you would prefer to invest in a mutual fund, then you should look at companies like T Rowe Price and the Principal Financial Group. These firms offer automatic asset builder plans that let you invest for $50 per month. You can buy stock funds, bond funds, or commodity funds.

5) Enroll in a DSPP. A DSPP is a direct stock purchase plan

which enables investors to purchase shares directly from the company. This investment service is cheaper than buying from a brokerage firm because investors avoid paying commissions. These plans often have low minimums that allow investors to automatically buy shares each month and reinvest dividends in the company automatically.

Getting Started Investing in Stocks

Online Discount Brokers for investors with smaller sums of money

www.buyandhold.com

No minimum to open an account.
Cost: $6.99 per month.
Includes 2 buy or sell orders a month.
Allows customers to purchase stock with as little as $20.

www.sharebuilder.com

No minimum to open an account.
No monthly fees.
Makes buying stocks in small dollar amounts affordable.
Cost: $4.00 to buy stock.
Only allowed to purchase stock on Tuesdays for the discounted price.

www.scottrade.com

$500 minimum to open an account.
No monthly fees.
$7.00 per buy and sell order.
Offers stocks, IRA's bonds, mutual funds, CD's.
No dividend reinvestment option.

www.etrade.com

$500 minimum to open an account.
Free dividend reinvestment plan.

Getting Started Investing

$9.99 per buy and sell order.
Lots of trading tools and research features.
Offers banking features, stocks, IRA's bonds, mutual funds, CD's.

www.tdameritrade.com

$2,000 minimum to open an account.
No monthly fees.
$9.99 per buy and sell order.
Offers banking features, stocks, IRA's bonds, mutual funds, CD's.

Chapter 9:

Saving For Your Kid's College

529 Plans

You should consider establishing a 529 plan for young children. Why is it called a 529 plan? The plan is named after the section of the Internal Revenue Service's code that authorizes these plans, Section 529. A 529 plan is an educational savings plan that is designed to help families set aside money for college tuition. 529 plans are federal government approved tax advantaged plans. These qualified tuition plans can provide special tax advantages such as state income tax deduction and tax deferred growth. This plan allows you to name yourself as the account holder and the child as the account beneficiary. This allows the account holder to ensure that the money will be used for the educational costs of the beneficiary. The two types of 529 plans are the college savings plans and the prepaid tuition plan.

College Savings Plans

College savings plans are investment plans that can be used at any college nationwide for most college expenses. In a college savings plan you select the appropriate portfolio based on your investment goals and risk tolerance. Your rate of return will vary based on your investment selection.

Plans vary from conservative to risky. Most college savings plans are managed by an independent mutual fund company. The good news is that most states allow you to deduct your contributions from your adjusted gross income which lowers your tax burden. For example in the state of Maryland, $2,500 of your contributions are tax deductible. The tax deduction applies to each beneficiary. So, if you were saving for 2 children in the state of Maryland than you could claim a deduction of $5,000. The bad news is that contributions are not eligible for federal income tax deductions. However, all earnings are exempt from federal income taxes as long as they are used towards college expenses. College savings plans give you the freedom to participate in another state's plan. If you are from the state of North Carolina and you like the Florida college investment plan better than your states plan, then you could enroll in Florida's plan.

Prepaid Tuition Plans

Prepaid tuition plans are savings plans that allow you to pay for future university tuition prices at today's rates. Under a prepaid plan, you make fixed payments for a fixed time period and the state guarantees the cost of college tuition when your child attends college. Today's payments lock in tomorrow's prices. Payments can even be applied to out-of-state schools, but the guarantee only applies to eligible in-state colleges. You are responsible for the difference in price if an out-of-state school has a higher tuition rate. Prepaid tuition plans may also be state tax deductible and earnings are free from both federal and state taxes. You can select a prepaid tuition plan that covers a minimum of one semester to a maximum of four years. Prepaid savings plans typically have age restrictions and require you to be a resident of the state in which the plan is established.

5 Things to look for when selecting a 529 plan

1) Compare plans across state lines.

Select the plan that best meets your needs regardless of location. Although you can invest in a 529 plan in any one of the 50 states, your best bet may be to invest in your home state's plan. Most state plans offer a tax deduction on contributions made to 529 plans. The catch is that that most plans require you to be a resident of the state to qualify. This tax break could allow a couple to deduct as much as $10,000 from your taxes. If you are going to invest in an out of state plan, be sure that the returns justify missing out on the tax deduction.

2) Decide between a prepaid plan and a college savings plan.

If you know that your son or daughter is going to attend college in state then go with a prepaid plan. Prepaid plans lock in tomorrow's tuition prices based on today's rates. You make a fixed number of payments for a number of years and your child's college tuition is guaranteed at any eligible state institution. Prepaid plans are only available to state residents. College savings plans are invested in mutual funds and rely more on investment growth to save or college. They have the potential for capital appreciation which would lessen the amount you need to save but they also have the risk of going down in value. College savings plans can be used towards educational expenses at any college nationwide but are not guaranteed to cover the cost.

3) Stay away from plans with high fees.

Pick a plan with low fees. Fees differ among plan providers. Some providers charge application fees, annual fees, asset management fees, transaction fees and low balance fees. These fees will eat up your returns over time. If you want to cut down on costs, consider a direct sold plan. Direct sold plans are bought directly from the plan's sponsor thereby allowing you to avoid paying sales fees. Adviser sold plans are typically bought from brokerage firms and they often come with load fees attached. Sales charges typically range from a modest 1% to an exorbitant 5.75%. Ouch! A 5.75% sales charge is a big hit to your overall return.

4) Pick a plan with a ton of investment options.

Be sure to pick a plan provider that you trust. Your management company should have an established history with a solid reputation. Look for a plan that has a nice mixture of fund offerings which will help provide you with diversification. For example, funds advisers like Vanguard and T Rowe Price offer stock, bond, index, and target date funds. Having more fund options will make it easier for you to build a portfolio that fits your needs. As your child gets older you will want to rebalance your portfolio from stock funds to bond funds. Target date funds do the heavy lifting for you by automatically rebalancing your portfolio annually. Be sure to evaluate the performance of the fund over the past 5 to 10 years.

5) Mix and match.

Are you still having a tough time trying to pick the right plan for you? Don't worry! You can pick more than one 529 plan. For example, if you don't like the options in your state's plan but want to take advantage of the tax deduction; you can invest in another state's plan as well. This gives you twice the investment options and the tax break. It's a win-win situation!

Saving For Your Kid's College

Chapter 10:

Teaching Your Kids about Money

This year make the decision to increase your child's financial IQ. Teach your kids about financial responsibility and proper money management skills. These lessons will last your child throughout their lives and into adulthood. It is important for them to learn about maximizing all of the financial resources that they have at their disposal. Listed below are some examples of ways that you can use to help familiarize your kids with financial concepts and investments.

Buy a savings bond.

You can teach your kids about money by investing in a savings bond. Savings bonds are a good starting investment because they are guaranteed to increase in value over time. Also, they are income tax free until redemption or maturity. Savings bonds can be purchased in paper form or electronic form from the United States government website (www.treasurydirect.gov). The bonds can be purchased in the children's names. The treasury direct website also enables you to open an account in your own name and buy bonds for the children as gifts. Savings bonds are available in $25 dollar denominations and accrue interest monthly.

Invest in a share of stock.

Another great idea for teaching kids about money is by investing in one share of stock. You can buy a young person one share of stock in a company that they love. For example, if your child loves Mickey Mouse, one share of Disney stock would be a great gift. For the child that loves computers, one share of Apple computer stock would suffice. Websites such as (www.oneshare.com) and (www.giveashare.com) are a great way to purchase stock for young people. These sites allow you to purchase a framed stock certificate with an engraved plague. A gift of stock can also help them become familiar with investing concepts at an early age. Each stock certificate comes with an owner's manual that explains exactly what it means to own stock in a publicly traded company.

Sign up for a custodial certificate of deposit.

A custodial certificate of deposit is an excellent way to teach your child the benefits of saving money. All funds in a custodial certificate of deposit are managed for the benefit of the minor. Custodial account certificates of deposit typically require much lower minimum balances than traditional certificates of deposit. Most major banks will allow you to establish a custodial account with your child. Some banks even offer add on certificates of deposit which allow the account holder to make additional contributions to the certificate over the term of investment.

Start a Roth IRA.

Your child doesn't have to be a full time working adult to start a Roth IRA. There is no age limit for a Roth IRA. If your high school student is earning income, they are eligible to contribute to a Roth IRA. What better way to teach your kid the value of saving than to show them how to save for their financial independence. The earlier that you get your child saving, the better their chances at accruing wealth.

Enroll them in a financial literacy program.

Many banks and credit unions offer financial literacy programs that teach young people the principles of financial management. Financial literacy programs teach teenagers how to build good saving habits for the future. They learn how to balance their checking accounts and techniques to avoid overspending. This is all useful information that will benefit your child in college. At the end of these programs, financial institutions often give away cash rewards and other prizes to all attendees. You can complete most programs in two or three weekends.

Create a budget.

Creating a budget is a great way to teach your son or daughter money management skills. Does your teen have a summer job lined up? Maybe they are cutting grass, working at the local movie theater, or working at a summer camp. No matter what the job is you can teach them to keep track of their income and expenses. Your teen will be able to see where they are spending their hard earned cash. You can either buy them a notepad or give them the gift of financial software. Quicken is one of the most popular personal financial management software programs. You can use free sites like the Mint.com or Wesabe. These sites will help you and your teen create a budget in no time.

Teach your teen to pay their own bills.

Prepare your child for the real world by having them start paying for their own clothes, cell phone bills, entertainment, etc. You can give them an allowance and let them see what it will be like to live off of a set amount of money. If they spend up all of their money then they can't make anymore purchases for the month unless they go out and earn more. They can do chores around the house or odd jobs to earn extra income. This is a great way to teach your child how to manage their bills.

Chapter 11:

Managing Credit

Individuals and small business owners alike have both been hurt by rising unemployment, limited access to capital, and a deteriorating economy. These factors have caused many people to lose their jobs and fall behind on their bills. Many people have plunged further and further into debt. How severe is this debt problem?

Mortgage Debt

According to the Center for Responsible Lending, there have been over 1 million foreclosures in the United States in 2009 alone. About 12% of all home loans are currently delinquent. Economists expect this number to double over the next 6 months. States such as Oregon have seen foreclosures rise approximately 90% this year. This is just the beginning. The government placed a moratorium on foreclosures last fall that stopped many of the banks from evicting homeowners until the end of March. Now that the moratorium has ended expect to see a major surge in foreclosures. Increasing job losses and decreasing home prices will lead to more foreclosures.

Credit Card Debt

While real estate may be the biggest debt culprit; credit cards are not far behind. I recently read a study that stated that the average American has over $8,000 in credit card debt. Credit card debt is a huge burden that affects most consumers. Credit card companies are in business to make money and not to help out consumers. They typically provide easy access to money at astronomical interest rates. Credit cards make it way too easy to overspend leaving consumers with massive amounts of credit card debt. According to the US Public Interest Research Group, between student loans and credit card debt, the average college student owes roughly $20,000 before they graduate and the average college freshmen has $1,300 in credit card debt, The average college senior has more than $2,600 in credit card debt.

As you can see managing credit is a problem throughout the United States. In this chapter we will take a look at some of the debt warning signs and discuss solutions to credit problems.

5 Signs that you are drowning in credit card debt

1) You use your credit card for survival.

You use your credit card so that you can pay your monthly bills. You use your credit card to pay for necessities like your phone bill, gas & electric or groceries.

2) You take out cash advances.

You depend on cash advances in order to make it through the month. Cash advances charge upfront fees, interest rates in the 20 percent range and have no grace period.

3) You don't know how much you owe.

You have no idea what your account balances are. You don't care to know how much you owe on your debts.

4) You don't open you credit card statement.

You have stopped opening your mail. You throw it in a drawer or in the trash. You would rather do anything than open your mail.

5) You avoid answering the phone.

You don't answer the phone. You know it is a bill collector calling about your debt so you don't even bother to pick it up.

How To Rebuild Your Credit

So, what can you do if you find yourself up to your neck in debt? Follow these simple steps to get on the path to rebuilding your credit.

1) Bring all new past due balances current.

Pay any new past due balances that have not yet negatively impacted your credit or been referred for collection. This will help stop any new judgments or wage garnishments. Sometimes just making a payment on a debt can keep it from being referred to a collection agency. The 1st step to rebuilding your credit is to head off those things that can drop your credit score even lower. Get every past due account below the maximum limit.

2) Examine your credit report.

Most unsecured debts that are at least 7 years old should be dropped from your credit report under the Fair Credit Reporting Act. Each state has a Statute Of Limitations (SOL) that states the maximum amount of time that a lender can seek to recover funds. Creditors can no longer sue you for collection of a debt once the SOL has expired. Collection agencies will continually try to collect old debts that you don't have to pay. Remember that companies will not request that negative information be dropped from your credit report so you have to. Alert your credit reporting agency that this old derogatory debt should be removed. Have any inaccurate information removed as well.

3) Negotiate with the creditors you owe.

This can be by phone, mail or email. I have always found letters the best way to communicate with lenders because there is a documented record on file. It also saves you from threats and harassing communication from creditors. Send your creditors a debt settlement letter letting them know what you are able to pay. Many creditors will take pennies on the dollar to settle an old debt. Companies write off delinquent accounts as a bad debt expense each year so any money that they receive is unexpected revenue. You may be able to settle a $5,000 credit card bill for $1,000.

4) Build new credit.

Once your past due debt has been paid up to date, now its time to start building good credit. If you don't have any open credit accounts then I recommend a secured credit card. Secured credit cards are cards backed by a deposit bank account. In order to get $500 worth of credit, you will have to deposit $500. Secured credit cards are good for people with no credit or bad credit. Buy one or two things and pay the balance off quickly. Keep the card for a year and you should receive offers for an unsecured credit card with a higher limit. Remember to pick a secured card with low fees and a decent interest rate.

5) Pay your new debts on time.

Pay all your bills within 30 days. If you want to have R1 credit it will take time. R1 credit is the highest credit rating and it means that you pay your accounts as agreed. You want to pay each debt as agreed with no late fee if possible. One trick I learned is that any debt that you pay within 30 days is reported as R1 even though the company may charge you a late fee. I do not recommend paying late fees but for those who juggle one bill to another it is worth knowing. After paying your debts as agreed for some time, you should be able to get an automobile loan from your credit union with a fair interest rate.

6) Maintain your good credit.

Keep your credit inquiries to less than two a year. At the most keep one unsecured credit card with little to no balance for emergencies. Keep your available credit higher than 70% on all of your accounts. By now your credit score should be good enough that you can purchase a home with a low interest rate.

This whole process may take time but after a few years your credit score should be much improved.

Credit Card Tips

At a time when banks are losing money due to toxic assets, they are dropping the hammer on the already pressured consumer. The credit card divisions of the major banks in the US are trying to make up for loan losses by increasing credit card interest rates. Banks are raising rates on customers regardless of payment history. Customers that pay on time have seen their credit card rates go up as much as 5% annually.

I find this behavior totally unjust. They should not be punishing customers who pay their bill to cover losses from customers who do not. This is a terrible business practice. So what can you do about it?

1) Stop using the card immediately.

You don't want to have future charges at the higher interest rate. It may be difficult now but you will be glad that you stopped charging in the long run.

2) Write a letter.

State your displeasure with the higher rate and request a lower rate. I used to call but calling can be a hassle. I found myself transferred to different customer service reps each time who knew nothing about my case. I write a letter when I have a complaint so that there is written documentation on file. I have gotten better results by writing a letter.

3) Be prepared to leave.

A lot of people threaten to leave their credit card company but do not follow through on it. If your credit card company refuses to lower your interest rate, it may be best to leave. They obviously do not value your business and you would do better to go elsewhere. Most credible companies hate to lose a loyal paying customer.

4. Transfer your outstanding balance.

If you have a solid payment history and decent credit score you will find a better rate. Check out websites such as bankrate.com. They offer lists of credit card companies nationwide and their current interest rates.

Chapter 12:

Biggest Money Traps

Every day millions of people are robbed of their hard-earned money due to expensive habits. Bad habits have a way of robbing you of your financial independence. If you want to build wealth, avoid these money traps.

Payday Loans

A friend of mine once told me about how he took out a few payday loans over a year ago. He said that he was strapped for cash and needed money in a hurry. He didn't want to ask friends or family so he went to a payday lender. He then proceeded to tell me a story of a never ending cycle of usurious interest rates, high processing fees and payments that kept him in debt for 16 months. He explained how a loan of $1500 ended up in a repayment of over $10,000.

When I heard his story I decided to look deeper into payday lending. I started by googling the phrase "payday loans". Over 5.75 million entries were returned by google search, I clicked on a few sites to do some investigating. To qualify for a payday loan you just need 2 forms of identification, bank statement, pay stub, personal check, social security number and a utility bill. That sounds simple enough. Payday lenders often refer to themselves as the quick and easy solution to your cash flow problems. Bad credit? No problem. Caught between paychecks? No problem. Short on cash? No problem. The problems come into play when you take a deeper look at the fine print in payday loan agreements.

    Payday loan websites make it as difficult as possible to determine the APR that they are charging. The most popular websites have interest rates ranging from 500% to a whopping 1630%. For every $100 borrowed many payday lenders will charge a "service charge" of $25 every two weeks. Let's say you took out a payday loan in the amount of $1,000. You would pay $250 biweekly to keep the loan active and none of this money would be applied to the principal. You would be making a $500 payment every month and not a dime would go to the principal of the loans. Payday loans have no maturity date and continue in perpetuity until you have enough money to pay more then the weekly service charge.

    The terrible part about payday loans is that they have onerous terms designed to prey upon the working poor that have bad credit. The interest rates offered are ridiculous. If someone is desperate enough to visit a payday lender for $1,000, what do you think the chances are that the same person will have $1,250 in two weeks to pay off the loan? Little to none. Most people just scrounge up enough money to keep paying the service charges to keep the loan active. If a person is fortunate enough to ever pay the loan off, they will likely find themselves in need of another payday loan due to the bad terms of the first loan. What payday lenders fail to tell people is that what many people believe to be a lifeline ultimately turns out to be an albatross driving them deeper and deeper into financial ruin.

Smoking

Smoking is one expensive habit to pick up. Not only is smoking bad for your health, it's bad for your wallet as well. Smoking raises the price of health insurance and decreases the money in your bank account. According to MSN Money, the average price for a pack of cigarettes nationwide is $5.00 and only getting higher. A pack of cigarettes is already costing $7.50 in Massachusetts and $10.00 in New York. If you smoked a pack of cigarettes a day, than you would be spending $35.00 per week. This would come out to $1,820 per year and over $54,000 over a 30 year period. That's assuming that cigarette prices stay stagnant, which we all know won't happen by a long shot. What could you do with an extra $54,000 dollars?

Gambling

Gambling comes in many different forms, but the end result is always the same. The house always wins. People gamble away their paychecks playing casino games, cards, online games, slots, and lotteries. Millions of people travel to Atlantic City and Las Vegas each year to gamble in casinos. Everyday people lose money playing lottery games such as Keno or trying to win the Mega Millions jackpot. A sad fact about lotteries is that the people that participate in them are always the ones who can least afford it. Low income individuals are the biggest players of lotteries. 82% of lottery revenue comes from low income individuals.

Gambling is an addictive habit that can end up costing you more than you bargained for.

Impulse Shopping

Have you ever gone in a department store looking to buy one shirt and left with bags full of clothes? While it's okay to splurge on occasion, it shouldn't become a habit. Most people engage in impulse shopping. Impulse shopping occurs when purchases are made out of emotion. A good example of impulse shopping is going to the mall and coming home with an item that you never planned on buying. Department stores count on shoppers making purchases due to impulse buying. Remember to always shop with a plan and to stay within your budget. An easy way to avoid impulse shopping is to only take enough cash for your preplanned purchase. That way if you are tempted to go over budget, your wallet will make the decision for you! Alternatively, you can make a list that you adhere to while shopping. This can really come in handy when you go to the grocery store hungry and end up buying everything that looks good.

Too Much Debt

The number one thing that keeps people from retiring is debt. Millions of Americans rack up huge amounts of debt due to auto loans, personal loans, and credit cards. The Federal Reserve measured consumer debt at a whopping $2.46 trillion dollars. And that doesn't even include real estate debt! The average credit card debt per household is over $16,000 according to Creditcards.com.

Alcohol

While drinking a glass of wine a day may lengthen you life expectancy, imbibing too much alcohol may kill your finances. With the average price of beer running $4, just drinking two bottles of beer a day can cost you $56 a week. That's almost $3,000 a year that could have been used to fund your retirement plan.

Biggest Money Traps

Chapter 13:

Money Saving Tips

25 Money Saving Tips

1) Skip the winter warm up.

Remember when you used to have to go outside and warm your car up during those cold winter mornings. Well, not anymore! Letting your engine idle is unnecessary for most modern cars. It puts excess wear on your engine and wastes gas. Just drive off slowly and don't mash the gas pedal.

2) Pack your lunch.

Eating out will eat a hole in your budget. It's expensive to eat out on a daily basis. It doesn't even have to be a 5 star restaurant for dining out to get expensive. $5 dollars here, $10 dollars there…..It adds up.

3) Cancel any newspaper and magazine subscriptions.

There is no need to order your hometown newspaper anymore. Today you can find the same information online for free. Just visit your favorite magazine or newspaper's website and start reading. You can even print out articles that you would like to have a hard copy of.

4) Skip the bottled water.

Switch to tap water. Not only are you saving the environment, you are saving money.

5) Skip the convenience store.

Do you regularly pick up items from your local convenience store? Do you pay your bills or get money out of the ATM at your local gas station? Convenience stores grossly overcharge you for the so called "convenience." Stores like 7-Eleven, Royal Farms, and Wawa's charge huge mark-ups on most food items, snacks, and toiletries. Convenience stores charge hefty transaction fees for routine services. ATM fees at convenience store can be as much as $3, plus your bank's fee. Bill payment services and money transfers also carry charges higher than most grocery stores.

6) Sell your fad collectible.

Remember when beanie babies were fetching ridiculous amounts of money. Not so today. If you have a valuable collectible sell it while it has some value.

7) Lower your gas and electric bill.

Following a few simple energy conservation tips can save you money on your home heating and cooling bills. Unplug electrical items (computers, cell phone chargers, and DVD players) when not in use. These items drain electricity and increase energy costs. Remember to turn off your air conditioner whenever you leave the house. There is no reason for the air conditioner to be blasting cold air when no one is there to enjoy it. During the winter turn the thermostat down. Turning your thermostat down 5 degrees in temperature represents a 15% savings. Make the switch to compact fluorescent light bulbs. These bulbs are better for the environment and cut down on energy costs.

8) Print your coupons.

If you're not already doing this, it's a great time to start! You can use coupons to save money on just about anything. Use them at your local grocery store or your favorite electronics retailer. Everyone knows that newspapers are a great place to start when searching for coupons. But there are also online sites that can help you save money like Coupons.com and CouponMom. You just enter your zip code and start saving. Also, be sure to check out the brand manufacturer's website. Manufacturers like Betty Crocker, Kellogg and Nabisco offer printable coupons on their websites. These savings can really add up over time. So take the time, get organized and start printing!

9) Do your Christmas shopping at troubled retailers.

Check out retailers that are in danger of going out of business. Troubled retailers have to liquidate their inventory. You can find some great deals at these stores facing tough times.

Money Saving Tips

10) Cancel your home telephone service.

Eliminate an unnecessary bill. Take advantage of the free nights and weekend plans for your cell phone. Now that you have a cell phone with unlimited services, you can get rid of your old landline service. It is possible today to survive without home telephone service. Landlines used to be necessary for alarm services. Not anymore. Most modern alarm systems offer wireless monitoring making a landline unnecessary. What if your cell phone service at home is spotty? If you get poor reception at home, consider a dual mode Wi-Fi cellular phone. Dual phones have the ability to make calls over both cellular and Wi-Fi networks. This should give you strong signal use from home. If getting rid of your landline service is not an option, than you can scale your service back. You can get a basic plan for $19.99 a month.

11) Avoid late fees.

Paying on time is not only good for your credit score but it also saves you money. Late fees are hidden fees that eat up your money. Do you want to pay your credit card bill late? No problem. Your credit card company will be glad to take your late payment. That's because the average credit card company will tack on a $35 late charge! Do you pay your gas and electric bill late every month? Utility companies will tack on fees ranging from $5 to $10 for late payments. Late cable and satellite payments will cost you another $5 dollars. Late cell phone payments will trigger a $5 late fee. All of these little late fees will end up costing you hundreds of dollars a year. Over a ten year time period these fees will end up robbing you of thousands of dollars.

12) Use more generic products.

Ditch the big name brands. You don't have to get rid of all brand name products but mix in some generics. Many grocery store brand generic products are of similar quality to the brand names. Generic aspirin has been found to work just as effectively as Tylenol, Bayer and other big name brands. Bread is often sold by big name manufacturers in generic labels. Sam's Club sells generic products under its Member's Mark brand and Costco sells generics under its Kirkland Signature brand. Your local grocery store has a plethora of generic brands. Why are generics cheaper? Generics are cheaper due to less advertising and marketing costs.

13) Use regular gasoline.

Visit your local gas station and you will see owner after owner putting premium fuel in their cars. Owners of different makes and models cars are ponying up for premium. Premium gas can cost anywhere from 20 to 40 cents more per gallon than regular gas. Why are so many people buying premium gasoline? The answer is because people believe that their cars run better on premium gasoline. This is a myth. The Federal Trade Commission and automobile manufacturers have stated that unless you have an automobile that specifically calls for higher octane fuel; there is no benefit to using premium fuel. So pump some regular gas and save yourself some cash.

14) Save your singles.

Lots of people have been taught from a young age to save their change. Quarters, dimes, nickels and pennies are saved in piggy banks. Adults can do the same thing by saving their dollar bills. Every day I take my dollar bills and place them in a jar. Then once a week I will go to the bank and deposit them. If I started the day with a 20 dollar bill and spent 6 dollars the whole day; I take 4 of the 14 dollars left over and save it. All 5's, 10's and 20's go in my wallet and I only save the singles. It's an easy way to build an emergency savings account without really feeling the hit.

15) Pay yourself first.

Did you pay someone in the past for your lawn and landscaping services? Did you get rid of your barber or stylist and decide to start cutting your own hair? Did you eliminate services from your cable company or cell phone provider? You should pay yourself every time that you eliminate a service that you used to pay for. If you were previously paying $50 for lawn care; than put $50 in your bank account whenever you cut your grass. If you can't afford to pay yourself the whole amount, then pay yourself at least half of the amount. This gets you in the habit of rewarding yourself when you make smart financial decisions. Would you rather have the money in your bank account or a company's bank account?

16) Use bank savings plans.

Take advantage of your banking institution's savings plans. Banks and credit unions often offer matching plans that will transfer money from your checking account to your savings. While I am not a fan of commercial banks, there are some good savings plans out there. For example, Bank of America's "Keep The Change" program rounds purchases to the nearest dollar amount and transfers the difference to your checking account. Bank of America matches 100% of the amount of the transfers for the first three months, then up to 5% every month thereafter. The maximum funds match is $250 per year. Wachovia has a similar program with its "Way2Save" plan.

17) Make saving automatic.

You can make saving easy by automating the process. Schedule small automatic transfers directly into your savings account. You can sign up at your local financial institution for part of your paycheck to be automatically deposited into your savings account. Some employers will even let you take money directly from your paycheck and deposit it in your savings for you.

18) Change your cell phone company.

Cell phone companies are lining up to compete for your business. You can save money by changing your current plan or switching to a new provider. Most major cell phone carries offer unlimited plans but the rates can be drastically different. T-Mobile customers pay $49.99 for unlimited calling. For $69.99 Sprint customers receive unlimited calling, internet access, text and picture messaging. AT&T recently announced a $69.99 plan that includes unlimited minutes. Verizon's unlimited plan is $99.99 and it cost $129.99 for web browsing and text messaging. A customer that switches from Verizon to Sprint would save $60 a month off of their cell phone service. That's an extra $720 a year. Be aware that there may be cancellation fees if you have a contract with your cell phone provider. You may be able to get out of your contract without paying a cent if your cell phone company has changed the terms of your contract. If you aren't able to get out of your contract, you can get them to prorate the amount that you owe based on the remaining months left in your contract.

19) Renegotiate your cable bill.

Although your paycheck may be decreasing, rates for cable television and satellite TV are steadily rising. Cable prices have been increasing 6 to 7 percent annually. According to the New York Times, cable prices have increased at twice the rate of inflation. So, how can you fight back against rising cable prices? Contact your local cable company and renegotiate your cable bill. Inform your cable provider that you are unable to keep paying such high prices. Major cable companies have customer retention departments. These customer retention departments will do just about anything to keep you as a customer including free months of service, price discounts, and lower annual rates. This is because it much cheaper for cable companies to retain a current customer than to pay the marketing costs associated with attracting a new customer. When negotiating with your cable company, always be prepared to cancel your service if necessary. You can always get a better price from a competitor. You may even discover that you can return to your former cable provider as a new customer and are eligible for new customer discounts.

20) Increase your insurance deductible.

Increasing the deductible on your insurance will decrease your monthly insurance bill. Car insurance and home insurance policies normally place your deductible as low as $250. While a low deductible means that you pay less out of pocket for accidents, it also means higher monthly payments. Insure.com estimates that raising your deductible to $500 will save you 12% and to $1,000 will save you 24% A good rule of thumb is to keep your deductible at $1,000. If you have a well funded emergency savings account, you should be able to cover any small accidents under $1,000. Besides when your insurance company pays a claim, your monthly rates are likely to increase as well. Do you really want to pay higher premiums for a $300 incident?

21) Save your gas money.

Use the extra money that you are saving on gas and place those savings in a high yield savings account. Gas prices have dropped sharply from their highs of this past summer. The average price for gas in my state has dropped from over $4.00 a gallon to $1.89. Just 6 months ago I was paying $75 to fill my gas tank up. Today $35 will give me a full tank of gas. I am taking the difference between what I used to pay for gas and what I am paying now and using it to build up my savings account. This tip can be used by anyone with a car. Pretend as if fuel prices are still $4.00 per gallon and deposit the extra money in your savings. This is a quick way to save some cash. So far I have been able to save $160 a month. Try it out. It works!

22) Save your raise.

Did you recently get a raise or a bonus at work? If so, what did you do with the extra money? If you aren't sure where it went, then it's the same effect as if you didn't get a raise. Start saving your raise. You were able to pay all of your bills before you got your raise, so keep doing the same thing. Take your extra raise and put it to work by increasing your 401(k) contribution or adding money to your savings account.

23) Increase your withholding allowances.

Do you look forward to getting a sizable tax refund every year? Getting a large tax refund is not necessarily a good thing. It is often a sign that you are overestimating your tax liability. Overpaying your tax liability is an interest-free loan that you are giving to the government. You could put that money to better use during the year by earning interest on it. If you increase your withholding allowance, the less you will have to pay in federal taxes. Many individuals that claim just one withholding allowance normally end up receiving a tax refund. The best use of your money is to pick the right number of withholding allowances so that you don't end up with a tax liability or a tax refund.

24) Get a savings buddy.

Just like you have a workout buddy, you can get a savings buddy! A savings buddy is a partner that will help keep you accountable about reaching your long-term savings goal. Your savings buddy will keep you motivated to make sure that you are sticking to your financial commitment. Let's say you have a goal of saving $200 a month. Your accountability partner will check in with you each month to make sure that you have contributed the $200 dollars. Your savings buddy will keep you encouraged during those months when you feel like slacking off. You are much more likely to stick to your goals with a financial accountability partner.

25) Ditch your debit card.

Whenever you need to make a purchase, drive to the bank and take out cash. I know that using a debit card or cash has the same effect, but the psychological effect is not the same. Swiping a card doesn't have the same mental impact as having to use cash. For example, if I am making a $200 purchase using my debit card, I find it easy to just swipe it and forget about the transaction. If I am using cash, however, I have to take 10 twenty dollar bills out of the bank, and think more about whether or not I really need to make this purchase. It is best to make it as inconvenient as possible to withdraw money.

Money Saving Tips

Holiday Savings Tips

The holiday season is the perfect time to discuss an issue that plagues just about each and every person, debt. During the Christmas season we use credit cards to charge electronics, toys, games, clothing and various presents. Many people buy items that they cannot afford or may not even need due to the allure of discounted prices. Bills created at Christmas don't just last during the Christmas season; these bills last year round. People spend 11 months or more paying off bills created over the course of a single month. Excessive buying at Christmas causes many individuals to declare bankruptcy in the first three months of the following year. So how can you avoid the debt trap during this holiday season? Follow these simple debt solutions

1) Have a plan and stick to it.

Before you hit the malls set a predetermined spending limit. No matter what happens do not go over your spending limit. Department stores and retail outlets count on shoppers making impulse purchases during the holidays. Avoid the impulse to buy items not on your list.

2) Stick to cash only purchases.

Only purchase items that you are paying for by cash or a form of cash. Debit cards, bank cards and check cards work well because they will typically keep you from spending more money then you have in your account. Remember you don't have to pay interest on money that is yours.

3) Minimize the dollar value of gifts.

Don't be Scrooge but be frugal! Remember Christmas is about giving, not about how much money you spend on presents. Allocate a specific amount to each person's gift that won't wind up putting you in the poorhouse in the New Year.

4) Avoid store credit cards offers.

One of the best ways to solve debt problems is by not creating any new debt. Stay away from store offers that promise huge discounts for signing up for a charge account today. These offers exist to entice you into spending money that you don't have. 15% off sounds good during the holidays but it doesn't sound so good when you are paying 23% interest on the bill in January.

Follow these simple steps and you can plan to go into next Christmas debt free.

Money Saving Tips

Chapter 14:

Money Making Ideas

1) Start a business.

One of the easiest ways to earn some extra cash is by becoming an entrepreneur. You can start your own business right from the comforts of you home for little to no cash. You could create websites for businesses that would like to advertise on the internet. Or maybe you would rather design logos for companies that need them. You could start an errand for hire business by running errands for busy working people and the elderly. There are numerous tasks from grocery shopping to picking up prescriptions that people would pay for to make their lives easier. Just look around and wherever you see a need you can create a business to fill it!

2) Sell your used and unused items.

A great way to make extra cash is by selling your items online. Sell your unused and used collectibles. You will get more money for unused items but you can sell used items online as well. Do you have old video games, DVD's, toys or books? All of these items are sold online daily. Do you make your own bracelets, t-shirts or key chains? You can sell just about anything online including handmade items. The most popular sites to sell items online are Ebay, Craigslist, and Amazon. Other lesser known sites are Half. com and Ioffer.

3) Become a freelance writer.

Do you have a passion and a talent for writing? If so, than become a freelance writer. There are many ways to get paid for your writing skills. Share your how to tips on Ehow. Are you passionate about any particular topic or interest? Start your own blog. As you build a following companies will pay you to advertise on your blog. Do you just want to work on specific projects? Become an independent contractor and write articles for elance. Write an e-book and market it to website owners.

4) Have a garage sale.

Sell all of your leftover items at a garage sale. A garage sale is the perfect place to sell all of those items that you couldn't unload online. Old furniture, clothes, tools, lawn equipment, and televisions can all be sold at a garage sale. Just hang up a sign and start selling! Not only will a garage sale unclutter your house; it will add a few bucks to your wallet.

5) Pick up a part time job.

A part time job provides reliable income. Do you have an interest in real estate? Become a home inspector. Insurance companies hire contractors to perform home inspections. All you need is a digital camera and reliable transportation. Do you have a car and a good driving record? You can deliver pizzas plus you get free food and tips. Even though full time jobs are scarce, part time jobs are readily available.
While none of these tasks are going to make you rich overnight; they are great ways to make some extra cash.

Chapter 15:

Great Financial Resources

7 Great Finance Books

The Intelligent Investor

The Intelligent Investor by Benjamin Graham is my favorite investing book of all time. Warren Buffett himself calls it "the greatest book on investing ever written." This book teaches you how to value any asset (stocks, bonds, real estate, and businesses). The Intelligent Investor's main premise is value investing. Graham teaches that financial markets are inefficient and investors can take advantage of this inefficiency by buying assets that are out of favor. Graham introduces a character known as "Mr. Market." Mr. Market makes you an offer everyday and you have to decide whether or not to accept Mr. Market's offer price. He stresses the importance of ignoring day-to-day fluctuations and only selling when your asking price is met. The book does tend to be a bit technical. It's not an exciting read, but the principles taught are timeless.

The Motley Fool Investment Guide: How The Fool's Beat Wall Street's Wise Men and How You Can Too

The Motley Fool is one of my favorite websites for investing information and the *Motley Fool Investment Guide* is one of my favorite books. It is written by David and Tom Gardener, the founders of the Motley Fool. The book teaches investing from a fun perspective and is easy to understand. The Motley Fool Investment Guide teaches all of the basic principles of investing and how to build a successful investment strategy. The Gardeners do a great job of breaking down financial terminology and investment options. This is a great read for the self directed investor. Also, check out The Motley Fool Investment Guide for Teens. I have found that the book contains a lot of useful information that the adults can benefit from as well.

One Up On Wall Street: How to Use What You Already Know To Make Money in the Market

The bestseller *One up on Wall Street* was written by Peter Lynch. Peter Lynch is the famed Fidelity mutual fund manager and noted philanthropist that made a fortune for his clients with the Fidelity Magellan Fund. Lynch advises investors to use their knowledge and personal experiences to find investment opportunities. Lynch's theory is to invest in businesses that you know. *One up on Wall Street* is built on the concept that the average investor can outperform the market. The average investor has an advantage over the market, because they can spot undervalued opportunities in their daily life. Many of Lynch's best investment ideas were found outside of Wall Street. It is an excellent book and is a very easy read.

The Dhandho Investor: The Low Risk Value Method to High Returns

The Dhandho Investor was written by Mohnish Pabrai. Dhando means endeavors that create wealth. Pabrai, a Warren Buffett disciple, is famous for once spending over $650,000 to have lunch with Warren Buffet. The Dhando Investor chronicles the principles that foreign investors follow to build businesses and generate wealth. Pabrai describes how the same principles used to become successful in the hotel/motel industry can be used in investing. Pabrai stresses the importance of investing heavily in your best ideas. His motto is "Heads, I win! Tails, I don't lose that much!" This is a newer book and an interesting read. The book is under 200 pages so you can read the whole book in one night.

Zero Debt: The Ultimate Guide To Financial Freedom by Lynnette Khalfani-Cox

Are you already in debt and plagued by calls from debt collectors? Then, you should take a look at *Zero Debt*. This is a very good book for digging yourself out of a financial hole. Zero Debt contains a practical financial plan that can be put into action right away. The book teaches techniques for dealing with pesky bill collectors and paying off past due debts. The Zero Debt plan teaches you lifestyle changes that will help you conquer debt and stay debt free for life.

Maxed Out: Hard Times in the Age of Easy Credit by James Scurlock

This is one of my favorite books because this book does an excellent job of explaining how the financial system really works. The book chronicles the abusive practices of credit card companies and how credit and lending are pervasive in all aspects of society. Our economy was fueled by lax lending standards and easy credit. A bubble developed with too many Americans living on debt, and the bubble burst when the bill came due. Now we are trying to recover from lifestyles that were fueled by debt. The amazing part is that this book was written before the economic collapse of 2008.

The Richest Man in Babylon by George Clason

The Richest Man in Babylon is an under appreciated classic. The book is a short read that contains excellent nuggets of wisdom. The Richest Man in Babylon was written from a Babylonian perspective and uses parables and principles to illustrate the importance of financial management. Self control and discipline are critical aspects to reducing spending and money management. My favorite principle is to never spend more than nine tenths of your earnings. If you only spend what you have, you will never go into debt.

Favorite Financial Sites

Bankrate (www.bankrate.com)

BloggingStocks (www.bloggingstocks.com)

Buy Like Buffett (www.buylikebuffett.com)

Businessweek (www.businessweek.com)

College Savings Plans (www.collegesavingsmd.org)

Credit Cards (www.creditcards.com)

CNNMoney (money.cnn.com)

FatWallet (www.fatwallet.com)

Forbes (www.forbes.com)

Google Finance (google.finance.com)

Investopedia (www.investopedia.com)

Investor's Business Daily (www.investors.com)

Kiplinger (www.kiplinger.com)

MarketWatch (www.marketwatch.com)

Mint (www.mint.com)

MoneyCrashers (www.moneycrashers.com)

Morningstar (www.morningstar.com)

Great Financial Resources

Motley Fool (www.fool.com)

SeekingAlpha (www.seekingalpha.com)

The Street (www.thestreet.com)

Yahoo Finance (finance.yahoo.com)

Works Cited Page

1. Motley Fool "A Bear Market for 401(k) plans" by Rich Duprey
http://www.fool.com/personal-finance/retirement/2008/03/18/a-bear-market-for-401k- plans.aspx

Great Financial Resources

Conclusion

I hope you enjoyed reading this book and learned a lot about the world of finance. In closing I would like to leave you with a plan of action known as The Ten Plays for Financial Freedom.

Ten Plays for Financial Freedom

1. Open a high yield savings account. Get rid of that low interest savings account and start earning a higher return on your money. Most financial plans start with a paying off debt strategy as number 1. It doesn't make sense to me to apply every dime of your money to getting out of debt if you don't have an emergency savings account. If you have no savings, you will end up right back in debt as soon as an emergency occurs. $2,000 is a good starting point for your savings account. Use some of the money saving tips in the book to reach this goal.

2. Double up on your debts. If you can't afford to pay off your debt, double up on the minimum payment. If your minimum credit card payment is $100, send $200. Doubling up on your payments will get you out of debt in no time. If you can pay more than this by all means, do it! Always pay the highest interest rate debt off first. It saves you the most money.

3. Max out your retirement plan. If your company offers a 401(k), your goal should be to take full advantage of

Conclusion

the matching plan. This is free money! If your company doesn't offer a 401(k), don't worry. You can start your own retirement plan. Check with your local bank or brokerage firm and open up a Roth IRA. You are now on your way to saving for retirement!

4. Fund your kid's 529 plan. It's time to start saving for Junior's college. Open up a 529 plan and make consistent payments every month. His eighteenth birthday will be here in no time.

5. Start investing on your own. Most retirement plans charge you a penalty if you want to take a distribution before 59 ½. If you want to retire early, open up a regular brokerage account with a discount broker. Start your portfolio off with a solid large cap mutual fund or large cap stocks. These are the anchors of your portfolio. They may not provide as much upside as riskier investments but they offer stability.

6. Add some fixed income. Bonds are a great way of getting a dependable income stream every 6 months. Pick up some highly rated corporate bonds. You can buy corporate bonds through most discount brokers. Another option is to pick up a bond fund. A bond fund will do the heavy lifting for you by selecting the bonds. High dividend paying stocks can also provide you with solid income. Companies like Verizon, Proctor & Gamble, AT&T, and ConocoPhillips have historically rewarded shareholders with high dividend payouts.

7. Add some risk to your portfolio. Now that your portfolio has anchors, let's add a motor. Pick up some small cap and midcap stocks. Do your homework and look for companies with growth potential and limited debt. Companies like Buffalo Wild Wings and Panera Bread have great growth

prospects and no debt. You could also pickup a small cap or midcap growth fund. Remember no single investment (stock, bond, mutual fund) can be greater than 20% of your overall portfolio.

8. Pay off your biggest debt. For most people their home is the largest debt that they will ever have. It may take 10 or 20 years but your long term goal is to pay off your home. Avoid constant refinancing and home equity loans. These loans will only make it more difficult for you to pay off your home loan. Think of it this way. A person who makes $100,000 a year and has $90,000 in annual debts actually has less money than someone who only makes $25,000 per year but is debt free.

9. Invest for the long run. Long term investors have the best chance at beating the market. Look at short term market drops as opportunities to buy more shares at a discounted price. Review the performance of your portfolio at least once a year but remember you are in it for the long run. Never buy a stock or mutual fund unless you are prepared to hold it for 5 years. This will help you keep your sanity during market downturns such as the market crash of 2008.

10. Live below your means. Create a budget and stick to it. Avoid buying status symbols such as mini mansions, luxury cars, and expensive clothes. Status symbols may make you look wealthy but they will leave you in the poorhouse.

Conclusion

Appendix

Your Financial Checklist

Summary of Assets

Name: _____   Date: _____

Instructions: Complete this form.

LIQUID ASSETS:

- **Cash and money market funds** $ _____
- **Certificates of deposit** $ _____
- **Brokerage accounts:**

   _____ $ _____

   _____ $ _____

   _____ $ _____

- **Other liquid assets**

   _____ $ _____

Total Liquid Assets $ _____

RETIREMENT ACCOUNTS:

_____ $ _____

_____ $ _____

_____ $ _____

OTHER ASSETS:

_____ $ _____

TOTAL ASSETS:
$ _____ $ _____

BANK ACCOUNTS

Bank Name	Checking, Savings, or Money Market	Avg. Balance
_____	_____	$ _____
_____	_____	$ _____
_____	_____	$ _____

CD's

CD's	Interest Rate	Maturity Date	Dollar Value
_____	_____ %	20 _____	$ _____
_____	_____ %	20 _____	$ _____
_____	_____ %	20 _____	$ _____

INVESTMENT ACCOUNTS

Account Held At	Account Type (Taxable, IRA, 401(k), 403(b), Annuity, etc.)	Dollar Value
_____	_____	$ _____
_____	_____	$ _____
_____	_____	$ _____

PERSONAL PROPERTY

	Estimated Value
Primary Residence	_____
Automobile(s)	_____
Other Real Estate	_____

LIABILITIES

Credit Cards	Interest Rate	Monthly Payment	Current Balance
_____	_____%	$_____	$_____
_____	_____%	$_____	$_____
_____	_____%	$_____	$_____

Debts (Home, Auto, Business, School)	Term	Interest Rate	Payment	Balance
_____	_____	_____%	$_____	$_____
_____	_____	_____%	$_____	$_____
_____	_____	_____%	$_____	$_____
_____	_____	_____%	$_____	$_____

What debts would you like to pay off over the next year?
_____
_____
_____
_____

What is your preferred asset class to invest in?
_____
_____

What is your financial goal? How many years will it take you to reach this goal?
_____
_____
_____
_____